# ART AND HISTORY
## OF
# PAESTUM

## THE EXCAVATIONS
## AND THE ARCHAEOLOGICAL MUSEUM

BONECHI

# INDEX

© Copyright    by Casa Editrice Bonechi, via Cairoli 18/b - 50131 Firenze - Italy - Tel. 55/576841 - Telex 571323 CEB - Fax 55/5000766
*All rights reserved. No part of this book may be reproduced in any form.*
*Printed in Italy by the Centro Stampa Editoriale Bonechi.*

Texts by: *Marina Cipriani* and *Giovanni Avagliano*
Translation by *Erika Pauli for Comunicare*
Photographs by *Gaetano Barone*: pages 5, 6, 8, 9, 10, 12, 13, 16, 17, 19, 20, 26, 27, 28 above, 30, 32, 33, 37, 40.
Photographs from the archives of the Casa Editrice Bonechi taken by *Rita Cerciello*: pp 14, 15, 18, 22, 23, 25, 28 below, 29, 31, 66-77;
The aerial photo on page 39 was taken by *Carlo Tripodi*; the photos on pp. 41-65 are by *Ferdinando Califano*.
Reconstructions and plan by *Stefano Benini*
The plan of the Heraion of Foce del Sele on p. 68 was kindly furnished by the Museo Archeologico Nazionale of Paestum.

ISBN 88-8029-077-0

*T*he ancient city of Poseidonia (later Paestum) lies in the center of the southern part of the plain of the Sele, built on a low travertine terrace once bathed on three sides by the waters of the river Salso (or Capodifiume). Finds of flint implements in the area of the great temples prove that the site was inhabited in the earliest stone age (Paleolithic). Traces of later settlements, of the Neolithic and Eneolithic periods (second millennium), were brought to light in 1960 in the vicinity of the Temple of Ceres. But the most significant evidence for this remote period comes from the neighboring Contrada Gaudo, about one km. north of the city, and dates to the Eneolithic period (first half of the second millennium B.C.). Vaulted tombs, excavated in the rock, contained the skeletons of several individuals, perhaps members of a single family group, accompanied by rough handmade pottery known as impasto, weapons and implements in flint or metal, evidence of the presence in the plain of Paestum, as in other areas of Southern Italy, of peoples from the Aegean-Anatolian area. Little is known of subsequent periods, even if faint traces in the area of the city and in the immediate surroundings prove that the site was never completely uninhabited, and relationships with the communities of Villanovan culture on the right banks of the Sele, with their principal center in Pontecagnano, are fairly well documented, at least on a material level, for the two centuries preceding the foundation of the Greek colony.

The foundation of Poseidonia, at the end of the 7th century B.C., was one of the last episodes of Greek colonization in southern Italy, which had begun in the 8th century B.C. with the foundation of Cumae. Then peoples from Achaea, a region in the north part of the Peloponnesus, founded the cities of Sybaris, Croton and Metapontum on the Ionian Sea towards the end of the 8th century. The complex historical events of the next one hundred years saw Sybaris at the center of a process of demographic and political growth and the foundation of Poseidonia was "the first political act of a project which projected the expansionism of the Sybarites of Sybaris over the Tyrrhenian". The geographer Strabo, who lived in the age of Augustus, describes the vicissitudes of the birth of Poseidonia as follows: "...The Sybarites then built a fortification on the sea, but the inhabitants moved further inland". Recent interpretation of this passage and present archaeological evidence seem to indicate that the installation of the colony involved the simultaneous occupation of three fundamental points in the territory: the promontory of Agropoli, where the sanctuary of Poseidon stood, the area of the city itself, and the sanctuary of Hera, 10 km. further north, near the river Sele which marked the boundaries with the Etruscan world.

Although Strabo and the few literary sources which mention the origins of the city (Pseudo Scymn. 244 ff.,Solinus II, 10) agree in attributing the foundation to the Sybarites, there is no hint as to just when this happened. However the tombs and the oldest material from the polis and the sanctuary of the Sele both seem to indicate some time around 600 B.C. as the most likely date for the birth of Poseidonia.

In any case it was during the 6th century B.C. that the city as such began to take form as it annexed the surrounding territory, destined from the beginning primarily for agriculture, the source of its great wealth. The first dwellings were built as well as various monumental structures in the urban sanctuaries, such as the shrine whose foundations still remain south of the Temple of Ceres and the archaic thesaurus at the mouth of the Sele River, from which the exceptional sculptural decoration in the Museum comes. Two invaluable documents remain to testify to the importance the city had acquired. The first is a bronze tablet found in the Sybarite thesaurus in Olympia, which informs us that Poseidonia stood surety for the alliance stipulated between its mother country and the Serdaioi, a people of whom nothing more is known. The second is a passage by the Greek historian Herodotus (I, 167) where none other than a citizen of Poseidonia sends the Phocaeans who survived the battle of Alalia (540 B.C.) to the land of the Oenotrians to found the city of Velia.

The economic prosperity and wealth achieved by Poseidonia in the last quarter of this century led to an intense building activity with the realization of the great temple buildings (Basilica, Athenaion) in the city and an urban layout of the streets, while in the territory the great sanctuary of Foce del Sele and the greater temple of Hera (see p.69) were built. It was also at this time that the agora, the square on which civic life centered, received its initial layout, a fact revealed by the discovery of the sacellum-heroon, which dates to the years 520-510 B.C. (see p.31) and marks the western limits. After the destruction of Sybaris (510 B.C.) by the Crotoniats, there was a reshuffling of the political and economical balance of power in the ambit of Magna Graecia and Sybarite exiles may at this time have found refuge in Poseidonia.

The first half of the 5th century B.C. was a period of great splendor for the city. By adopting a new system of coinage, modelled on that of the Sybarites, Poseidonia hoped to play a role of prime importance in trade with the rich internal regions as well. Unfortunately written texts of this period contain no mention of events which concern the city, except for the naming of one of its athletes, Parmenides, who in 468 B.C. won the stadium competition in the 78th Olympic Games.

Yet there must have been events of far-reaching significance within the political-institutional setup of the city, for how else could one explain the existence of a building recently excavated, a bouleuterion, which rose inside the boundaries of the Greek agora in 480-470 B.C. to house assemblies of at least 500 persons, a sign of the existence of a political regime with a certain amount of popular representation. The so-called temple of Neptune was also built at this time.

Historical information, provided once more by

Strabo, leads us to the second half of the century: in the course of a war with Velia (won, however, by Velia as a result of the good laws it had received from the philosophers Parmenides and Zeno), Poseidonia fought side by side with the Lucanians. This is the first indication of the presence of this Italic peoples, and just how well organized they were, including the waging of war.

By the second half of the 5th century B.C. the Samnites were ready to undertake the conquest of the Greek and Etruscan cities of Campania, and the Lucanians, around 400 B.C., to take over Poseidonia. Tradition says little about just when and how this happened but archaeological documentation helps fill in the gap: traces of fire in the sanctuary of Hera at Foce del Sele and a conflagration, followed by a restoration, around 400 B.C. inside the temple of Ceres, speak in favor of a violent conquest towards the end of the 5th century B.C. In the cemeteries the funerary traditions changed and the simple burials of Greek type, with only a few objects or even with no tomb furnishings at all, disappeared and were replaced by tombs with weapons and rich furnishings, often decorated on the inner walls by funerary paintings of strictly Italic tradition (see p.58 for the painted tombs on exhibition in the Museum). Study of these archaeological documents gives us a general idea, in the absence of written sources, of the social organization of this community, which also took over the surrounding fertile territory as shown by the many farms. In the city, where the great temples and principal buildings of the Greek period continued to be used, new monuments were added to the public area. For example, two large porticoes were erected along the borders of the agora and the southern sanctuary. Monuments of later periods (see p.31) now cover all traces, while nothing is known concerning private edifices of this time. The assembly hall of Greek times was still used, as shown clearly by an inscription in Oscan, the language of the Lucanians, set up on the tiers of the Greek bouleuterion and which, in a dedication to Jupiter, furnishes us with the name of the magistrate Statis.

The historical events of the second half of the 4th century B.C. see Poseidonia involved in the military operations connected with the arrival in Italy of Alexander the Molossian, king of Epirus and uncle of Alexander the Great. Called by the Tarantines to fight the Bruttians, Samnites and Lucanians, he arrived as far as the city walls. It is not certain whether or not he occupied Poseidonia, but if he did it was certainly only very briefly.

Subsequently the city was involved in the events of the Second and Third Samnite Wars, in which the Lucanian confederation fought side by side with Rome against the Samnites. In the following war of Rome against Pyrrhus and the Tarantines, the Lucanians however sided with the latter and were punished, after their defeat, with the loss of Poseidonia. In 273 a Latin colony was installed here which took the Italic name of Paestum.

Although the great temples were preserved intact, romanization led to a profound and radical change not only in the layout of the city with the creation of the Forum square and those civic and religious monuments which were part of all Latin colonies, but also in the territory, where traces of a regular agrarian subdivision, a requisite for distributing the land to the new colonists, has only recently come to light.

The city played an important role in the war between Rome and Carthage. In 216 B.C., the most difficult moment of the Second Punic War, ambassadors from Paestum offered Rome golden vases from the sanctuaries to sustain the war effort. The Roman Senate thanked Paestum but did not accept the offer (Livy XXII, 36, 9).

After 210 B.C., the colony continued to support the Roman cause, furnishing, as once more narrated by Livy, ships for the fleet as well as continuous proof of loyalty to Rome, so as to merit, together with 17 other Latin colonies, public praise in the Senate (Livy XXVII, 10). The effects of the general crisis which hit all of Southern Italy after the end of the Punic Wars and which caused impoverishment and depopulation of the ancient cities almost everywhere, must also have been felt in Paestum. After the Social War (1st cent. B.C.), the colony became a municipium and, shortly thereafter during the Servile War, in which the slave Spartacus challenged Rome, its territory was the site of clashes between the Roman troops and the rebels. Except for a modest resumption of building activity in the time of the emperor Augustus and an increase in the population as a result of the installation in Paestum, in 71 A.D., under the emperor Vespasian, of a colony of veterans from the fleet stationed in Misenum, no events of great importance seem to have occurred in the imperial age. Signs of its slow but progressive decline were by now evident and became irreversible in the course of the 4th and 5th centuries of our era, when the inhabited center, consisting of mean structures built with reused material, was concentrated around the ancient Athenaion, transformed into a Christian church. Information on Paestum in the early Middle Ages, when the city was the seat of a bishopric, is not yet forthcoming. Sometime between the 8th and 9th century the site was almost completely abandoned by its few inhabitants who, as new forms of settlement were affirmed, fled from the waters of the plain, which were no longer regulated, and moved to the coast of Monte Calpazio, giving life to Caputaquis, which replaced Paestum as the dominant center of the territory.

Ever since, even though Neapolitan circles of the 16th and 17th centuries showed signs of interest in the Paestan antiquities, an understanding of their true meaning was something the times were not yet ripe for. Not until the innovative climate of the mid-1700s did European culture "rediscover" Paestum and realize how important the innovations presented by its temples were for the study of ancient architecture. The parts of the city brought to light in about 200 years of excavations and studies, and open to the public, correspond only to the central strip of the ancient town. The remaining area, even though clearly marked by the walls, is still in private hands and practically unexplored. There is a sacred area at each end of the archaeological park: the northern sanctuary, centered around the temple of Athena, better known as the temple of Ceres, and the much larger southern sanctuary, with the Basilica and the temple of Neptune. The large open area between the sacred zones was, from the beginning of the city's life, reserved for public life, first with the meeting place of the Greek agora and then, further south, the Forum of the Roman city. Areas for private use, a number of city blocks, dating to the Hellenistic-Roman layout, have been uncovered prevalently in the strip to the west of the large paved Roman road, running in a north-south direction.

*The Roman road leading in a north-south direction ("Via Sacra"). In the background, to the right, the Temple of Neptune.*

Porta Sirena.

The city walls, southern side.

The city walls with the tower on the southeast corner.

# PAESTUM

## THE WALLS OF PAESTUM

Paestum is surrounded by a circuit of walls, almost completely preserved, about 4750 m. long, which follows the course of the travertine shelf on which the city stands. This double curtain wall of large squared blocks is filled in with earth while towers are set at intervals along its polygonal perimeter. The four principal entrance gates open in corrispondence with the cardinal points: there are also a series of 47 lesser openings, known as *posterulae*, which served both as points of access to the city and in the organization of defense. Porta Sirena, or Siren Gate, whose name derives from the imaginary creature sculptured for apothropaic purposes on the outside of the gate itself, is on the east. Two square uprights have been preserved as well as a round-headed arch above the opening. To the left of this gateway, looking from the outside in, there is an opening up high

for a Roman aqueduct which brought water to the city.

On the south side is the Porta Giustizia (Gate of Justice), with a spacious entrance vestibule, defended on either side by towers, one round and the other square. A few arches of a small bridge in blocks of stone still stand outside this gate. The bridge forded the waters of the Capodifiume, which had been deviated into a moat at the foot of the wall as additional protection.

Entrance to the city from the side facing the sea was through the Porta Marina which also had a spacious paved vestibule defended at the sides by two square and one circular tower.

Little remains of the Porta Aurea (Golden Gate) to the north of the city, demolished early in the nineteenth century when the road which still unfortunately cuts through the ancient center was built. It was also protected by two towers, a round one on

West facade of the Temple of Neptune.

The interior of the Temple of Neptune: the southern peristasis.

On the following pages:
the Temple of Neptune seen from the northeast.

the east, a square one on the west, and it was preceded by a bridge over the moat, the remains of which can be seen in the escarpment below the road. Almost all the 28 towers in the circuit of walls have been completely destroyed or reduced to ruins. The two fine square towers to be seen on the SE corner and on the southern side are on the whole the result of a nineteenth-century restoration.

The chronology of the walls of Paestum is still under study. Obviously the present aspect of these fortifications is the result of a series of modifications, including layout, variations in building techniques, additions and restorations which range from the 4th century B.C. well into the Roman period. Indeed the addition of architectural decorations in various points is documented as late as the 1st century B.C. Subsequently the walls, no longer strategically important, were used as burial sites for the last inhabitants of the city.

The visitor may also wish to drive around the entire circuit to see just what its defensive preparations were like and to get an idea of the area covered by the city. The entrance adjacent to the Temple of Neptune leads directly into the southern sanctuary of the city, containing numerous sacred buildings and religious installations, such as shrines, altars and votive deposits, where the gifts the faithful offered to the divinities were kept. The sacred area is dominated by the mass of the two large Doric temples, the Basilica and the Temple of Neptune, a good starting point for the visit.

## TEMPLE OF NEPTUNE

The best preserved of the temples of *Magna Graecia* is the Temple of Neptune, so-called because it seemed logical that the most imposing temple in the city had been dedicated to the god for whom the city was named - Poseidon/Neptune. The temple stands on a *crepidoma* (base) of three steps and has six columns on the facade and 13 on the long sides. Thanks to its perfect state of preservation, almost all the constituent parts and their precise proportional relationship can be observed, thus making it an ideal model of the Doric temple of the classic period.

The columns, in local limestone and almost nine meters high, are only slightly narrower at the top

The Temple of Neptune: detail of the western facade.

The Temple of Neptune: detail of the south side.

than at the base, while the swelling in the central part, the entasis, much more pronounced in the columns of the older and adjacent Basilica, is relatively slight.

There are all of 24 flutes which help to make the columns seem more slender. At the top, each column is marked by three deep horizontal incised grooves (necking-grooves) to which four rings in relief or necking bands correspond on the echinus above. The first element of the entablature, the architrave formed of two blocks set side by side, rests on the abacus, the square slab which is set above the capital. It is decorated above by a projecting band (*taenia*) from which *regulae*, or narrow projecting strips recur below each triglyph, decorated below by six "drops" (*guttae*), or cylindrical pegs, carved in stone. The upper part, which consists of the alternation of metope and triglyph, constitutes the Doric frieze.

Above each metope and every triglyph, can be seen a projecting horizontal element, like a crowning cornice, decorated on the underside by rectangular divisions in relief (*mutuli*). On the projecting part these elements carry three regular rows of six guttae, which may have been in the form of a truncated cone, separately carved and inserted into holes made expressly for the purpose, of which only the empty spaces are visible. This technique can also be observed close up on a block that has fallen from the crowning cornice and now lies along the south side of the temple.

On the short sides the triangular pediments are framed by the *geison* cornice with an extremely simple molding. No signs of holes, clamps or dowels are to be seen in the tympanum, or pedimental slab, thus apparently excluding the existence of a sculptured pediment decoration.

Cavities of various sizes and square in shape can be noted on many parts of the building, such as columns and pilasters. They indicate the points in

13

14

The Temple of Neptune: detail of the entablature of the southeast corner.

The Temple of Neptune: detail of the architrave, the abacus and the corner capital.

The Temple of Neptune: detail of the Doric frieze.

which defects in the building material were filled in with plugs of the same material. But in ancient times these repairs were not visible for they were covered by the layer of white stucco which was applied to the structures, sometimes accentuated by lively bands of black, blue and red.

Inside, the cella fits into the plan of the *peristasis* according to a precise geometric relation, and is preceded by a pronaos composed of two columns between anta pilasters which supported a true frieze composed of metopes and triglyphs. A high step leads from the *pronaos* to the *cella*, which has a small room on either side of the entrance, enclosed by walls, where the stone stairs which led to the upper parts of the temple were housed and of which a few fragments still exist. All the blocks of the perimetral walls have been removed from the cella. The paving of the cella is composed of bands of three slabs each, but in one place towards the back

there are only two. One hypothesis is that this was where the cult statue was placed. A double row of seven columns divides this space into three aisles, and since it was so high, a second order of columns was required, some of which are still preserved together with their architrave, to support the ceiling. The complex framework of the roof rested on the numerous niches which can be seen from the inside in the upper parts and in the back part of the two short sides, and which served as housing for the five mighty principal beams.

On the opposite side, to the west, is the *opisthodomos*, also preceded by two columns set between pilasters. Originally it obviously did not communicate with the cella and the opening there now is due to the subsequent despoilment of the temple.

While the inside ceiling of the temple was in wood, outside it had a gable roof, perhaps covered with

The eastern facade of the Temple of Neptune.

Temple of Neptune: detail of the western side.

marble tiles. No decorative architectural elements which can with certainty be referred to this building exist however.

In front of the east, or principal, side is an entrance ramp added in Roman times, and there are two altars in addition to various bases for statues and votive offerings. Nothing is left of the older and larger altar, built in large blocks of limestone, except the foundations also cut by a channel. It was replaced in Roman times by a smaller altar, situated nearer the temple entrance. In addition to the foundations, molded portions of the base of the podium are still extant.

A series of particular technical and optical expedients was employed in building the temple of Neptune in order to improve and exalt its visual impact. Here let it suffice to mention the slight curvature of the horizontal lines, visible for example on the plane on which the columns stand.

For a long time this temple has been considered, on the basis of formal analogies, as being slightly later than the temple of Zeus in Olympia, designed by the Elean Libo and erected between 471 and 456 B.C. while more recent studies set it entirely within the evolutionary process of temple architecture in the Greek West and in Sicily in the second quarter of the 5th century B.C., in which significant elements of autonomy in the design have been identified.

Scholars do not agree as to the identity of the divinity worshipped here: in the past both Hera and Zeus had been considered, while recent studies, stressing the relationship which seems more than casual with the layout of the temple buildings of another great Achaean city of Magna Graecia, Metapontum, refer the monument to the cult of Apollo.

The Basilica and the Temple of Neptune seen from the southeast.

The western facade of the Basilica.

The Basilica: detail of the colonnade.

On the following pages:
the eastern facade of the Basilica.

# THE BASILICA

The Basilica stands to the south of the temple of Neptune, at the southern extremity of the sanctuary, near the walls. The structure received its present name in the 18th century when Paestum was being "rediscovered", for the fact that there were no pediments together with the elevated number of columns on the short sides seemed to indicate a building for civil use and not a place of worship.

This is the oldest of the Paestan temples still standing, and construction, begun around the middle of the 6th century B.C., lasted approximately thirty years. During this time various modifications were carried out on the initial project. The *peristasis* has 18 columns on the long sides and no less than 9 on the fronts, resting on a stylobate preceded by two steps. The shafts of the columns in the perimeter of the *peristasis* display the characteristic swelling (convex enlargement), or *entasis*, in the central part, and have 20 broad shallow flutes with a slightly sunken band in the upper part, creating a striking effect of light and dark, with a crown of vertical leaves which leads into the *echinus* above. Some of the capitals on the western side, in particular, have a rich decoration of plant motifs in relief on the echinus as do the columns in the *pronaos* and inside the *cella*. It should be noted that all the capitals are in limestone, except the one at the south-east corner, which is in sandstone. Above the architrave, which consists of large blocks of limestone (inside, the sockets for housing the ceiling beams can be observed), there is a continuous band in sandstone, decorated both inside and out with moldings similar to those on the temple of Ceres (a detail that can also be noted on the fragments on the ground, south of the building). The surviving elements of the frieze and the upper parts have led to the hypothesis that the Basilica had a frieze of metopes and triglyphs, carved separately and probably in sandstone, while, thanks again to the study of the fallen fragments, the presence in the upper parts of other courses in sandstone, also decorated with moldings, has been hypothesized.

A great number of the elements of the rich polychrome terra cotta decoration of the roof, renewed more than once, are on exhibit in the Museum.

The interior arrangement is strictly connected to that of the peristasis: the cella, open on the east, is preceded by a pronaos composed of three columns, set between two pilasters (also with entasis), surmounted by elegant anta capitals. Inside, a row of columns running down the center was part of the original plan, and an opisthodomos or room opening only towards the opposite side, with a central column, was at the other end. Subsequently this room was closed and became an *adyton*, or inner sanctuary, reached only from the cella. This may be when the level of the cella floor, of which part of the original paving has been preserved, was raised, to which the fact that, where the slabs are missing, the base of the central columns is below the pavement, bears witness. Only three of these columns (probably originally seven) are still standing. The first two have sandstone capitals, while the size and fine decoration can be observed on the capital that has fallen to the ground.

It is important to note that during construction, the central colonnade which divided the cella in two was always preserved, although from a point of view of statics this expedient was not strictly necessary. It is therefore highly likely that a double cella was a cult requirement. The votive offerings found in the deposits near the building on which the attribution of the temple to Hera is based, also revealed that the goddess was worshipped here both as a warrior goddess (worshipped by men alone) and as the goddess who supervised the birth and growth of the individual. Some scholars, although they accept the hypothesis of a dual cult, propose the divine couple Hera-Zeus: the latter would also have had another building dedicated to him, which must have stood on the site of the present temple of Neptune.

In the Roman republican period, the roof of the basilica was once more renewed and Juno, who corresponds to Hera in the Latin pantheon, may also have been worshipped there. The semicircular entrance steps, flanked by bases, is an addition from Roman times. The rectangular altar, with three steps leading up to it, stands in front of the temple, aligned with the facade and preceded by several bases meant for votive offerings. At present the altar appears higher because excavations have also uncovered part of the foundations.

*The Basilica: detail of the southwest corner of the elevation.*

*The Basilica: detail of the capital on the southeast corner.*

*The Basilica: detail.*

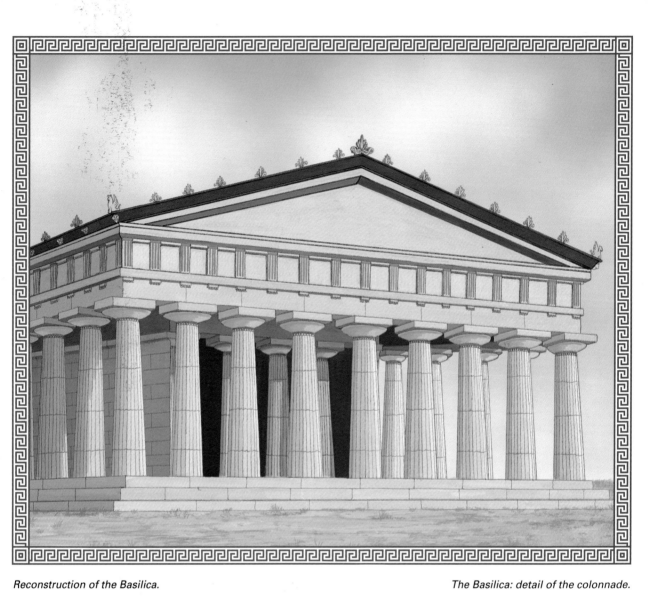

*Reconstruction of the Basilica.*

*The Basilica: detail of the colonnade.*

*The Roman road leading in a north-south direction
("Via Sacra").*

# VIA SACRA AND RESIDENTIAL QUARTERS

Behind the temples, to the west, the foundations of the long wall, built in blocks of stone, which enclosed the sanctuary, are encountered before arriving at the Roman street, with its large paving stones, conventionally called the Via Sacra, which leads from Porta Giustizia to the Forum. Continuing along this street towards the Forum, on the left are the dwelling quarters of Roman times, organized in long blocks, divided into two rows of houses separated by an inner wall. In their ground plan, unless variations were introduced in the course of the centuries, the houses are of the traditional Hellenistic type, with atrium, impluvium and peristyle. At the intersection with the other main street which leads to the Porta Marina, the houses in one of these blocks, recently restored, can be visited, or one can begin the visit to the monuments of the Forum.

# THE MONUMENTS OF THE FORUM

The original layout dates to the 3rd century B.C., in other words, to the period of the Latin colony. At present the square, whose eastern side is beneath the modern road, is surrounded by a portico with columns and capitals from other older buildings, some of which were set up in the early 1900s.
The *tabernae*, rectangular shops divided into two rooms and sometimes with an upper floor, opened off the sides of the portico. A building with three niches in the back wall is to be noted on the west side, between the *tabernae*. It has been identified as a Lares shrine (3rd cent. A.D.).
The row of *tabernae* on the southern side of the Forum is interrupted by a large building generally known as the Curia, composed of a central hall surrounded on three sides by a portico that was originally covered. The large central area, its walls articulated with niches and attached columns, contains a stone exedra. The monument has been identified as

*The interior of the so-called Curia.*

a Basilica, the place where justice was administered, and which was built in the 3rd century A.D. on the remains of precedent buildings, including another basilica of the Augustan period and a Greek temple of the late 6th century B.C. of which parts of the foundations of the front are visible under the adjacent *Macellum*.

This building (3rd cent. A.D.) stands to the east of the so-called Curia and was entered from the Forum by means of a staircase in which elements from an altar of Italic type were reused. It served as a covered market.

Two other monumental buildings are fitted into the sequence of shops on the north side: the *Comitium* and the Italic Temple. The former, circular in form, with steps supported by an artificial embankment, has obviously been cut by the podium of the temple, which is therefore more recent.

Excavations have proved that the *Comitium* was erected immediately after 273 B.C. by the first generation of Latin settlers of Paestum, to house the assembly of citizens called to elect the magistrature. Aside from the difference in size, it is modelled on the *Comitium* of Rome, which was repeated also in other Latin colonies established in the same years as Paestum, such as *Cosa* and *Alba Fucens*.

# THE ITALIC TEMPLE

The Italic Temple, known also as Temple of Peace, was not part of the original project for the Forum. Excavations have indeed proved that it was erected in the 2nd century B.C., and even partially cut into the *Comitium*. Set on a high shaped podium, it was surrounded by columns (except in the back) which had Corinthian capitals with large acanthus leaves and female heads at the corners. A few extant examples lie on the floor of the podium. The cella inside the colonnade may possibly have been divided into three rooms (although this has not yet been verified), leading to the hypothesis that the temple was a *Capitolium* and was therefore dedicated to Jupiter, Juno and Minerva, the divinities of the Capitoline triad. Recent studies make it seem more likely that the building was consecrated to *Mens* the divinity-symbol of the gratitude of the freedmen towards their masters and therefore, of the gratitude of Paestum to Rome. The extant metopes have recently been placed on the western side of the podium. Decorated with scenes of battle between warriors armed in Greek style and excitedly running female figures, they evoke the modes and forms of early Hellenistic sculpture.

27

The Italic Temple.

Detail of the metopes of the Italic Temple.

The western entrance to the Amphitheater seen from inside.

## PISCINA

After leaving the Italic Temple, right behind the *tabernae* of the northwest side of the forum, is an area traditionally thought to be a gymnasium, occupied in great part by a large pool (47 m. long and 20 m. wide), originally surrounded by an enclosure of large blocks.

This has recently been identified as the sanctuary of *Venus Verticordia*, built by the Latin colonists in the 3rd century B.C., at the time the Forum was first organized. The cult of the goddess (as we know above all from Ovid who described it in detail) included a ritual bath of the statue of the goddess. Subsequently women who hoped to propitiate fertility or a successful childbirth bathed collectively in the same waters.

This interpretation of the monument is also supported by the presence, not only of the remains of the enclosure in blocks of stone, a real sanctuary peribolus, but by the existence, in the northeast corner of the pool, of an access ramp used in the processions and by an ashlar base on the western side, presumably for a wooden pedestal, used in the rites.

## AMPHITHEATER

Passing back behind the monuments of the Forum and turning east, is the Amphitheater, of which only the western portion is visible. The rest is in part cut by Via delle Calabrie, built by the Bourbons in 1829, and in part is still on privately owned land.

The monument was built in the 1st century B.C.. between the age of Sulla and that of Caesar, in squared limestone blocks. The brick piers, visible along the outer perimeter, were added when the building was enlarged and served to support a second order of tiers, perhaps at the time of the Flavian emperors, when a colony of veterans was established in Paestum. Entrance to the arena, in which the surviving tiers and the vaulted corridor where animals and equipment for the spectacles must have been kept and which can still be seen, is through the western gate, which however has a vault that is not original and is the result of an unfortunate attempt at restoration dating to the 1960s.

*Details of the residential blocks dating to Roman times.*

*The Heroon on the agora of Poseidonia ("Hypogeum Shrine").*

# AGORA

A portico to be seen immediately to the north upon leaving the amphitheater bounds the southern side of what was once the agora, the public space of the Greek city. It originally stretched from this portico to the northern sanctuary and, in an east-west direction, from the so-called Hypogeum Shrine up to the area at present occupied by the Museum. With the building of the Forum when the city was romanized, the square ceased its functions and, after a period of semi-abandonment, was turned into a residential area in imperial times. The remains of houses can be seen here. Today two of its principal monuments are there for us to see: the first, the so-called Hypogeum Shrine or Underground Sacellum, is to be found on the eastern side of the paved Roman street. Surrounded by an enclosure in blocks added under the Romans, this singular monument, dated to 510 B.C., has no openings. Almost square in form, sunk into the rock shelf and covered by a gabled roof, it is actually a cenotaph-*heroon*, the symbolic tomb of the founder of Poseidonia, who after his death became the object of a hero cult, which found its natural site in the square where the city's political life unfolded. This interpretation is comforted by the material found inside the monument (reached by removing part of the roof) and which consisted of

eight bronze vases filled with honey, five large spits resting on two blocks set side by side and a black-figure Attic amphora which, quite reasonably, presents the scene of the apotheosis of Hercules, the hero par excellence.

# BOULEUTERION

On the other side of the agora square, practically facing the Museum, is a circular building dug out of the rock in a series of concentric tiers, orginally faced with blocks which served as seats, of which only a few are still in situ. This was the building where assemblies of about 500 persons (the calculated capacity) were held and therefore seems to have been the *bouleuterion* of the city, built in circa 470 B.C. and still functioning, despite the fact that the political and institutional picture had changed, during the Lucanian period, as witnessed by a dedication of the magistrate *Statis* to Jupiter, found in place in the cavea.

After the founding of the Latin colony and the building of the *Comitium*, a sanctuary, of which part of the enclosure and a fountain are visible, was built on the site of the *bouleuterion* which had been filled in with stones and earth after an expiatory sacrifice.

*The Temple of Ceres: eastern facade.*

# TEMPLE OF CERES

Still further north, on the other side of the agora, lies the north sanctuary of the city, dominated by the building commonly known as the temple of Ceres. To be seen here, in addition to the foundations of an archaic temple (580 B.C.), are the remains of a portico, the altar in front of the temple, and in the back, to the right of the latter, an isolated column reconstructed in modern times. The temple, attributed to Ceres by 18th-century scholars, was really dedicated to Athena, as proved by the numerous statuettes of the goddess, shown armed (helmet, aegida, a small mantle covering her shoulders and torso and bearing a Gorgon mask, the shield) that were found in the votive deposits around the building. An inscription dedicated to Minerva, the goddess who corresponds to Athena in the Latin pantheon, affirms the continuity of this cult in Roman times.

The temple, which is soon to be completely restored, was built around 500 B.C. and is an outstanding example of temple architecture for the period of transition between late Archaic and the dawn of classicism.
The elegant structure characterized by the marvelous balance between plan and elevation can best be perceived by walking completely around the *peristasis* of Doric columns (6 on the short sides and 14 on the long sides) which are slenderer than those of the Basilica. Inside, the cella or *naos*, or at least the foundations thereof, are clearly visible. A spacious portico (*pronaos*) originally preceded the cella. The *pronaos* had six Ionic columns, with capitals in sandstone (many have survived, now outside the temple, and two capitals are on exhibit in the museum), and served as entrance to the actual cella,

32

*Temple of Ceres: interior.*

*On the following pages:
reconstruction of the Temple of Ceres.*

*On pages 36,37:
the Temple of Ceres seen from the northeast: in the
foreground, on the left, a base and the column
re-erected in the 1950s.*

a spacious hall with a harmonious finely proportioned interior, where the statue of the goddess was kept. Two monumental staircases, of which the traces lie hidden in the thick walls between the *pronaos* and the *naos*, led to the upper zone of the temple. This would seem to imply that worshippers participated in the rites enacted in the most holy part of the temple, seat of the simulacrum of the divinity, contrary to information gleaned from ancient literary sources, which describe the temples as off bounds to the practices of collective worship, which took place outside, near the altar.

The details of the elevation of the building merit particular attention: the capitals of the exterior Doric colonnade are decorated with crowns of leaves in relief, originally colored alternately red and blue and enriched here and there with applications of gilded bronze lamina, as was revealed recently when the column on the SE corner was cleaned. The heavy entablature, in better condition only on the pedimental sides, consists of a smooth architrave of blocks set next to each other, with a sequence of border moldings in relief, some of which in sandstone, above which is the frieze of metopes and triglyphs (the latter in sandstone). The raking cornices of the pediments (on the eastern one the brick restoration of 1828 is more visible) were decorated beneath with coffered sinkings, the oldest extant example; rosettes and stars in sandstone were applied to the center of every coffer with lead clamps. A few elements can be seen under the shed to the west of the temple. The rest of the gutter cornice with lion-head spouts can be admired together with other architectural elements from the building in the room in the Museum dedicated to the entire northern sanctuary.

In late antiquity, as indicated by the medieval tombs still to be found inside the southern *peristasis,* the temple seems to have been transformed into a Christian church to meet the religious needs of the remaining inhabitants of the abandoned city who had created a small village (wiped out in the 1950s) here on the heights, right up against the ancient place of worship.

35

The Temple of Ceres: details of the eastern pediment.

Bird's-eye view of the northern sanctuary.

The Temple of Ceres: detail of the eastern pediment seen from below: note the only triglyph in sandstone still extant.

Tomb furnishings from the tomb of a Lucanian man.

# THE MUSEO ARCHEOLOGICO NAZIONALE

The Museo Archeologico Nazionale of Paestum was founded in 1952, on the basis of a questionable choice, at the center of the ancient city, as part of a general project by M. De Vita dating to 1938. An exhibition for the public in embryonic form already existed in the adjacent bishop's palace. In precedence objects that came to light were sent to the National Museum in Naples or the Provincial Museum in Salerno. The original nucleus was the first room, laid out in line with the dimensions of the structure on which the metopes of the first *thesaurus* of Foce Sele are displayed, allowing for two points of view, from below and from the balcony of the upper gallery. But before long the mass of finds which came to light in the city and the rich necropolises by far exceeded the capacity of this container, a building in the style of the architect Piacentini.

Less than twenty years after its inauguration. E. De Felice designed a first enlargement of the original nucleus, consisting of the room for the architectural fragments from the greater temple of Foce del Sele, with a series of new rooms, characterized by an itinerary around an internal garden with ample windows opening towards the outside.

G. De Franciscis (aided by S. Viola) set up the present museum installation in the new rooms, and, in part, the old ones, with an itinerary centered on various focal points (rooms of the sanctuaries, of the Diver, of Lucanian painting). The exhibition criteria which have come to the fore in recent years where stress is laid on environmental conditions, safeguarding of the integrity of the objects on exhibition and the need of furnishing visitors with information that will aid in understanding what is seen, will probably lead to variations in the itineraries and in the exhibition of some of the most important finds. It is therefore deemed best here to deal with the Museum collections as such and with some of the most interesting pieces, independently of the actual itinerary, where they will however be easy to identify.

41

# SCULPTURES FROM THE HERAION OF FOCE DEL SELE

The two large rooms on the ground floor house the rich architectural and sculptural decoration from the excavations of the *Heraion* of Foce del Sele (p. 69) and a wide array of architectural fragments and ex-votos, in prevalence terra cottas with the image of the goddess Hera or of offerers, but also vases, objects in metal and bone, offered by the faithful during the long life of the sanctuary. There is also a bearded bronze head, from a statue of the latter half of the 4th century B.C., perhaps a philosopher or a priest, which came to light by chance in the waters of the Sele. The archaic metopes in sandstone (570/60 B.C.) were attributed by the original discoverers to the first *thesaurus* and therefore mounted on a structure which supposedly copied the original structure in height and size, thus gravely conditioning any hypothesis for future installations in the Museum. The discovery in 1959 of three more metopes of the same cycle, now exhibited on a balustrade below to the right of the so-called *thesaurus*, has raised serious doubts as to the validity of this reconstruction, making it much more likely that they once decorated and protected the upper

*Heraion of Foce del Sele: metope with Heracles killing a giant.*

*Heraion of Foce del Sele. Greater Temple: metope of the frieze with the dancing maidens.*

Heraion of Foce del Sele. The Greater Temple: fragments of the decoration of the sima and the cornice.

Bronze head from the river Sele.

part of the wooden beams of more than one building. Executed in different techniques (relief or outlining of the figure in silhouette) by various sculptors, the metopes depict episodes from the Greek myth and *epos*. Eighteen are dedicated to the feats of Heracles (Hercules) whose very name ("renowned through Hera") indicates his close bonds with the goddess of the sanctuary. Others are dedicated to episodes from the Trojan war or themes of the story of Orestes, inspired by literary traditions elaborated in the Greek West early in the 6th century B.C. The other room on the ground floor houses the lion-headed rain spouts and the ten surviving metopes of the greater temple of the *Heraion*.

The metopes (510 B.C.) are strongly permeated by Ionian figural culture, and form a sort of continuous narrative, showing a row of maidens, moving in pairs towards the right, while only one appears to be fleeing with her head turned backwards. Just which myth is depicted (rape of Helen ? flight of the Nereids frightened by the struggle between their father and Heracles ?, etc.) depends on how the movements are interpreted.

## PREHISTORY AND GAUDO

Flint implements, found east of the Basilica early in the 1900s and datable to the Paleolithic period, constitute the oldest evidence for the presence of man on the site where Poseidonia was later to rise.

The materials of the culture known as Serra d'Alto, near Matera, (roll handles) and of Diana (in the Aeolian Islands; fragments of cups, jars, bowls, spool handles), which come from an excavation carried out in 1960 northwest of the temple of Ceres date to the Neolithic period. The objects that accompanied burials (such as cups and bowls decorated with incised short lines) from the same area bear witness to contacts with the Eneolithic culture of Laterza in Puglia.

But the most conspicuous complex of Eneolithic material on exhibit comes from the area of Gaudo (see p.3), with funeral furnishings which include weapons of flint, or more rarely, metal, implements in ossidian and shiny black pottery vases. The most common forms are pitchers with a globular body, cylindrical neck and vertical handles, the so-called "salt dishes", double vases where the two elements are connected by a bridge above which is a handle, and the square or triangular shaped *askos*. All these forms compare to examples from the Aegean and Anatolian world.

Material dating to the Iron Age is scarse: the small necropolis of Capodifiume (9th cent. B.C.), east of the city, bears witness to the presence of a nucleus of farmers, who belonged to what is known as the Villanovan culture, an offshoot from the neighboring center of Pontecagnano, and who placed the ashes of the deceased in biconical impasto amphoras covered with a large bowl.

*Heraion of Foce del Sele. Thesaurus: metope with Heracles and Deianeira.*

*Heraion of Foce del Sele. Thesaurus: metope with Heracles and the Cercopes.*

*Eneolithic cemeteries of Gaudo: details of some of the pottery found in the tombs.*

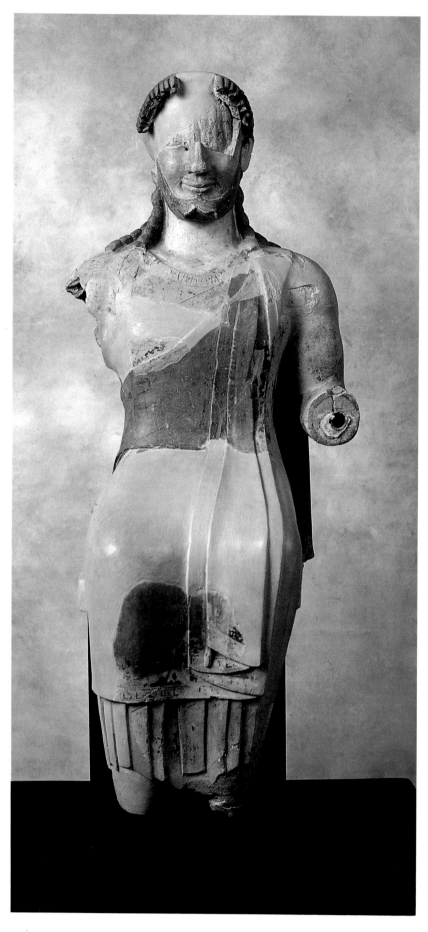

## OBJECTS FROM THE URBAN SANCTUARIES

A sampling of the oldest import- ed pottery, above all Corinthian (late 7th cent. B.C.), so far found in Paestum opens the rich section dedicated to the city. The greater part of the collection consists of objects from the urban sanctuar- ies, in which the cults of the *polis* are reflected. In addition to the great number of statuettes, the votive deposits have also yielded polychrome terra cotta sculptures of great beauty, which have been compared, on various grounds, to contemporary Etruscan work.

Among these of particular note is a cult statue of a male divinity on a throne (Zeus?) which must originally have been in a shrine in the southern sanctuary. Datable to around 520 B.C., the figure has a rather massive body, covered by a yellow chiton and a red cloak bordered with geomet- ric motives in black. The face and the nude parts are painted bright red: the beard, the thin moustache and the hair (on which a bronze crown, now lost, must have rested) set in small vertical ringlets on the forehead and gath- ered together at the back in large tubular braids which fall heavily behind the shoulders, are in black.

*Terra cotta cult statue, perhaps Zeus.*

The headless female bust, her dress decorated with swastikas, must have been an architectural decoration. This piece too (500 B.C.) displays a preference, as in the Zeus, for full robust forms, which emerge from under the thin garment marked at the waist by a wavy border.

## BRONZE VASES FROM THE HEROON

The most important nucleus of bronze objects in the city consists of the six *hydriai* and the two amphoras from the *sacellum-heroon* of the agora of Poseidonia. Their attribution to one or more centers of production in Southern Italy is still a question of debate.

The amphoras are undecorated and only the smallest one has handles with a hand-shaped termination. The handles of the *hydriai*, on the other hand, are richly decorated: female heads with long braids, flanked by reclining rams, lions which grasp the edge of the vase, crouching sphinxes and horse's heads. A splendid lion in the round, standing erect on his hind legs, serves as the vertical handle of the finest and most original *hydria* in this group.

*Terra cotta female bust, probably a decoration from the elevation of a cult building.*

*One of the bronze hydriai from the Heroon on the agora.*

*On the following pages: Attic black-figure amphora from the Heroon on the agora.*

*Figurines and busts in terra cotta from the votive deposits in the southern sanctuary.*

*Terra cotta statuettes from the southern sanctuary: on the left the image of Hera Eileithya.*

47

Detail of a terra cotta bust from one of the repositories of the southern sanctuary.

Terra cotta statuettes from one of the repositories of the southern sanctuary: on the left woman-flower.

## PAESTAN CERAMICS

A large quantity of red-figure painted pottery, produced by the pottery workshops in the city, was present in the tomb furnishings of the Lucanian period. Recent studies have now made it possible to date the beginning of this activity to around 380 B.C. The finest examples of this production can be assigned to three painters. We know the names of two, *Assteas* and *Python*, because they were the only potters in Magna Graecia who signed some of their works. One of the finest vases signed by *Assteas* is a *hydria* with the depiction of the departure of Bellerophon for Lycia, found in the tomb in Contrada Vecchia in Agropoli.

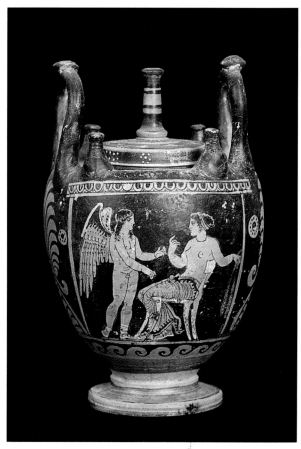

*Paestan red-figure lebes gamikos.*

*Tomb furnishings from a Lucanian tomb.*

But a *lekythos*, unsigned, from tomb no. 2 of Contrada Gaudo, with the theme of the purification of Orestes at Delphi, is also attributed to this painter. *Python*, perhaps a pupil of *Assteas*, signed the large painted amphora in tomb no. 24 of the necropolis of Andriuolo, which bears a lively picture of the birth of Helen from Leda's egg, shown on a polychrome altar on the base of which are painted the words "Python egrapsen" (Python painted).

The third outstanding artisan, who however did not sign his work, is known as the *Aphrodite Painter*, from the subject depicted on the large polychrome amphora of tomb no. 13 of the

*The main side of the amphora by the Aphrodite Painter showing the goddess between two erotes.*

Licinella. On the main side of the vase, Aphrodite is shown between two erotes. The goddess holds a timbal in her left hand and emerges from a complicated leaf motif which spreads out in tendrils, leaves and flowers over the entire vase. On the back is Dionysus in a rustic landscape, surrounded by maenads and young satyrs with offerings, thyrsus staffs and garlands of flowers. The *oinochoe* (also in tomb no. 13), with the judgement of Paris into whose presence Hermes is leading Hera, Athena and Aphrodite, is also by his hand. The goddess of love is seen from the front, before the other goddesses, indicating that she will win the contest.

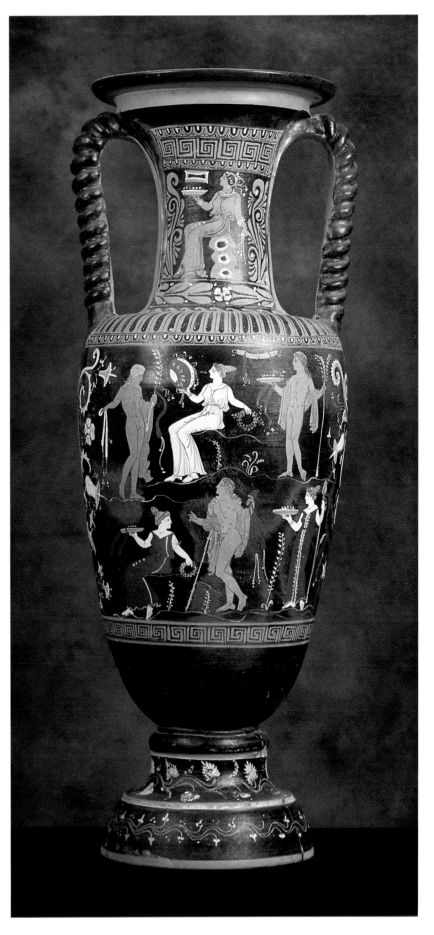

*The back of the amphora by the Aphrodite Painter: below Dionysus between satyrs and maenads.*

54

*Interior of a Paestan red-figure kylix.*

*Tomb furnishings from a Lucanian tomb.*

*Paestan red-figure hydria from the workshop of Assteas.*

*Paestan red-figure kraters.*

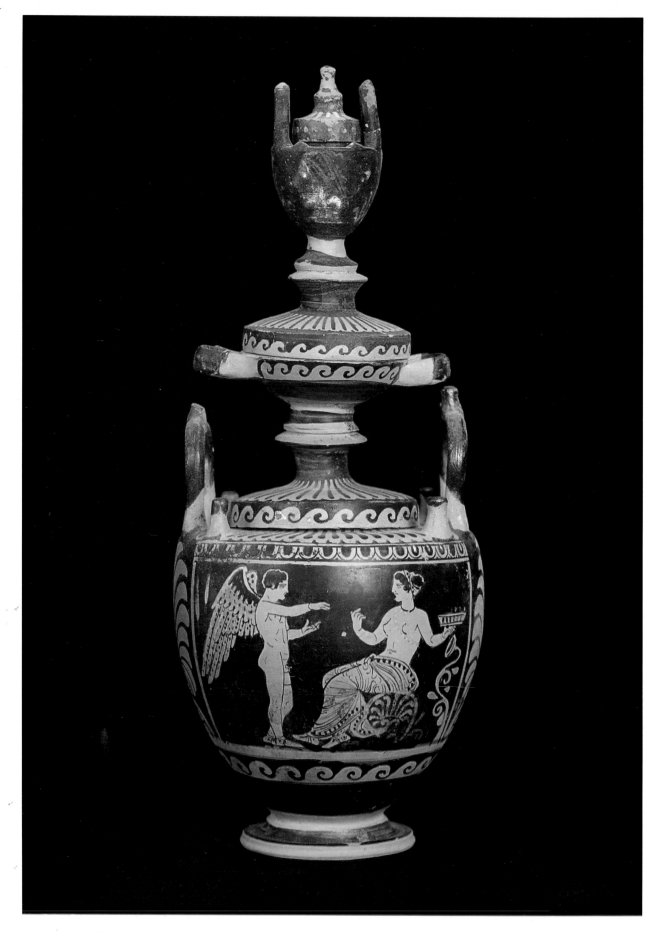

# MARSYAS

The bronze statue of the silenus Marsyas, found in the Forum of Paestum in 1931, on the other hand takes us to the moment of the founding of the Latin colony (273 B.C.). The small armless figure, bearded and so squat as to seem swollen and almost deformed, consists of five detached parts, separately cast and joined together. He is wearing sandals and has open shackles (*compedes*) on his ankles. The most likely hypothesis sees Marsyas as the symbol of the liberty the new colonists of Paestum who were of plebeian origin had achieved.

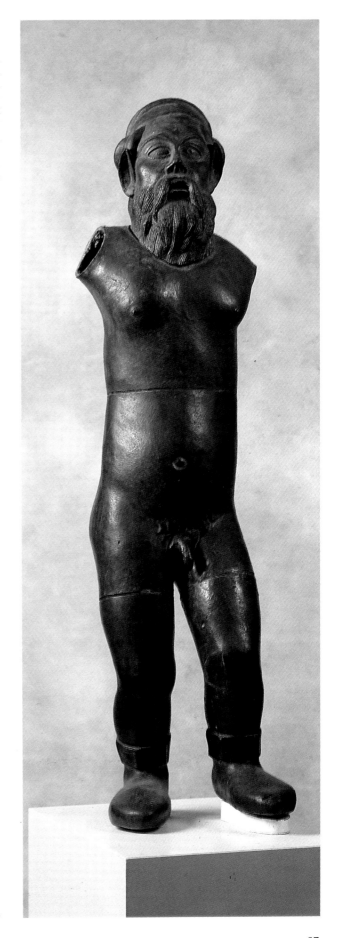

*Paestan lebes gamikos consisting of several parts.*

*Bronze statue of the silenus Marsyas.*

# THE PAINTED TOMBS OF THE 4TH CENTURY B.C.

While painted tombs were foreign to Greek culture (in this sense the Tomb of the Diver is an unicum), with Lucanian dominion the custom spread in Paestum in the 4th century B.C., although it was always the prerogative of the rising classes. The rich series of funerary paintings date to this period, but the limited space available permits the exhibition of only a small part, recently restored.

The tombs are a cassa, that is in box form, and, as revealed by the triangular shape of the slabs on the short sides, had a gabled roof. Analysis of the paintings, abetted by the study of the material laid into the tombs with the deceased (there were sometimes dozens of vases, weapons for the men, jewelry for the women: a panorama quite unlike the sobriety of the Greek furnishings), makes it possible to follow the development of this art throughout the 4th century B.C.

The oldest tombs, which can be dated around 380/370 B.C., are decorated in the central space of the slab with bands, garlands, bands or sashes, branches and sometimes representations of objects actually placed in the tomb with the body. A good example of this group is tomb no. 21 from Andriuolo with bushes and birds. Around 360 B.C. actual figures began to appear. In the largest group the main slab depicts a warrior on horseback, his helmet decorated with feathers and a cuirass consisting of three disks of Italic type, welcomed by a woman who hands him the vessels for drinking, as in tomb no. 12 from Andriuolo. This scene is found only in the tombs of men. In those of women the principal slab bears decorative elements, such as pomegranates and garlands. The images on the other sides of the box, for members of both sexes, depict duels, boxers, chariot races, in other words the funeral games in honor of the dead, documented for the Roman world by the historian Polybius.

After the middle of the century a precise iconography was elaborated for female burials as well: the woman is shown either alive, spinning wool, or dead, on her funeral couch, surrounded by mourners, as on the western slab of tomb no. 47 of Andriuolo.

In the last quarter of the century, the figures are as tall as the slab and new symbolic motifs appear: battles between panthers and griffons, friezes of weapons, winged Victories on chariots.

*Painted tombs of the Lucanian period: the slabs of the long sides of tomb no. 58 in the necropolis of Andriuolo.*

*On the following pages: tomb no. 58 in the necropolis of Andriuolo: short west side and short east side.*

60

# THE TOMB OF THE DIVER

A special room in the Museum has been dedicated to the so-called Tomb of the Diver, which has recently been restored (1987).

It is a simple burial, a cassa, consisting of slabs, closed by a flat lid, decorated with frescoes on the inner walls. The sober furnishings included the remains of a lyre with its sound box made of a tortoise shell and a black-figure *lekythos* which helps date the deposition to 480/470 B.C., a period also indicated by the style of the painting. The short wall on the left hand side shows a nude youth holding a pitcher and standing next to a large krater from which he is about to dip wine. On the long walls is a scene of *symposium* (a Greek party): banqueters with garlands of leaves, reclining alone or in couples on *klinai* are shown playing *kottabos* or engaged in amorous conversation, while a drunken banqueter embraces a zither-playing ephebus, or listening enraptured as one of them plays the double flute. On the other short side, a youth, accompanied by an older man, leaves the symposium preceded by a flute player.

Painted on the lid, right over the deceased, is a nude man diving into a body of water. The scene is symbolic: the dive is to be interpreted as the passage from life to death. The pylon in the foreground to the diver's right (and which is not a diving board) has been identified as the marker set at the limits between the known world and the river Oceanus (the body of water into which the man is diving), which the ancient Greeks believed led to the subterranean realm of the netherworld. In a recent reinterpretation of the monument, the pylon has been identified as the gateway to Hades, comparing it with analogous representations on vases painted with the scene of Ulysses travelling towards the Infernal Regions.

The Tomb of the Diver is the only 5th century B.C. example of funerary painting in Poseidonia and is also an interesting document of the contacts that existed between the Greek city and the Etruscan world, for the custom of painting the internal walls of the sepulcher recalls ritual customs more widespread in Capua and Etruria.

The work has been attributed to two artists of different caliber (freer and more sure the painter of the diving scene, who also did the slab of the *kottabos* players and the two lovers), both evidently well acquainted with the techniques and conquests of contemporary Greek painting, which must however have been of much higher quality and which has been completely lost.

*Tomb of the Diver: the north wall and the south wall.*

*Tomb of the Diver: the short west wall and the short east wall.*

*Tomb of the Diver: the covering slab; reconstruction of the tomb.*

65

# THE CHURCH OF THE SS. ANNUNZIATA

In the small square near the Museum stand the 18th-century Palazzo Vescovile and the church of the SS. Annunziata, first built as a cemetery basilica in the 5th-6th century A. D. The original structure, which consisted of a single apsed hall, preceded by a quadriporticus, was enlarged in the 12th century in Romanesque forms, with the interior divided into a nave and two aisles by two rows of reused ancient columns and with the addition of two side apses. Fragments of 9th-century frescoes are visible below on the oldest part of the central apse, while the angel above belongs to the subsequent phase. The interior of the church, formerly renovated in Baroque style, was recently restored to its original forms.

*Paestum, Church of the SS. Annunziata.*

*Paestum, Church of the SS. Annunziata, interior.*

*Sanctuary of Getsemani: statue of Christ praying in the Garden of Olives.*

# THE ENVIRONS OF PAESTUM

Near the road that leads to the modern town of Capaccio are the springs of Capodifiume, the stream which bathes Paestum, highly evocative and of naturalistic interest. At the center of the spring structures of Roman times, perhaps traces of a nymphaeum, are to be seen.

The ruins of a castle, the circuit of walls and the towers of the medieval town of *Caputaquis* lie above, on the spur of Monte Calpazio. Probably founded in the 9th century A.D., after the old city had been abandoned, it was wiped out in 1248 by Frederick II of Swabia. The inhabitants moved to the nearby hamlet of S. Pietro, which later became what is now Capaccio, with its typical 18th-century lanes and noble palaces with rich sculptured portals.

The plain of Paestum however continues to be dominated by the imposing church of S. Maria del Granato, probably erected in the 12th century (although remains of an earlier church can be seen near the entrance) with a three-aisle Latin cross interior and apses along the sides. After recent work, the ancient cathedral, restored in 1708 and 1836, has an austere interior, with reused antique columns and capitals. Not much is left of the original pavement, decorated with marble tesserae. Frescoes with a scene of martyrdom (14th cent.) can be seen below a marble pulpit with polychrome decoration and supported by three small columns, while S. Biagio in bishop's attire (15th cent.) is depicted on the supporting wall at the side. The church takes its name from the image of a Madonna venerated here who has a pomegranate on her scepter. In the past this iconography has been interpreted as a sign of the continuity through the centuries of the cult of the Argive Hera who appears holding the same fruit in many Paestan terra cottas of the classic period.

A few km. from the Church of S. Maria del Granato stands a modern religious complex, known as Getsemani. In the crypt of the futuristic church is a life-size, highly mystical statue of Jesus praying in the Garden of Olives.

## AGROPOLI
Agropoli, an old small town of the Cilento, is only a few km. south of Paestum. The historical center, a characteristic nucleus of unplanned architecture, also contains the remains of the so-called Saracen Castle, in memory of a long period of Arab settlement here (882-1028). It is highly likely that the Greek sanctuary of Poseidon lies under the castle. Remains of architectural terra cottas which decorated a 6th century B.C. temple, found in recent excavations, seem to confirm the felicitous intuition of Paola Zancani Montuoro in 1954.

## THE CAVES OF CASTELCIVITA
The modern town of Castelcivita has a tall circular tower dating to the 13th century, which has an escarped base with a fluted motif, reminiscent of the Castelnuovo in Naples in its Angevin phase, and with a series of pointed arches above.

The town owes its fame primarily to the caves nearby, one of the finest and most important karstic complexes in Southern Italy. Although known in the 18th century, not until the 1920s were the caves scientifically explored. Recent work on the entrance and the installation of a modern lighting system inside facilitate the visit to this evocative site. Tunnels and rooms of varying size can be admired along the route of circa 1700 m. The most spectacular of these bizarre limestone formations are indicated with picturesque names: the precipice, the leap, the great cascade.

*Castelcivita (near Salerno): entrance to the caves.*

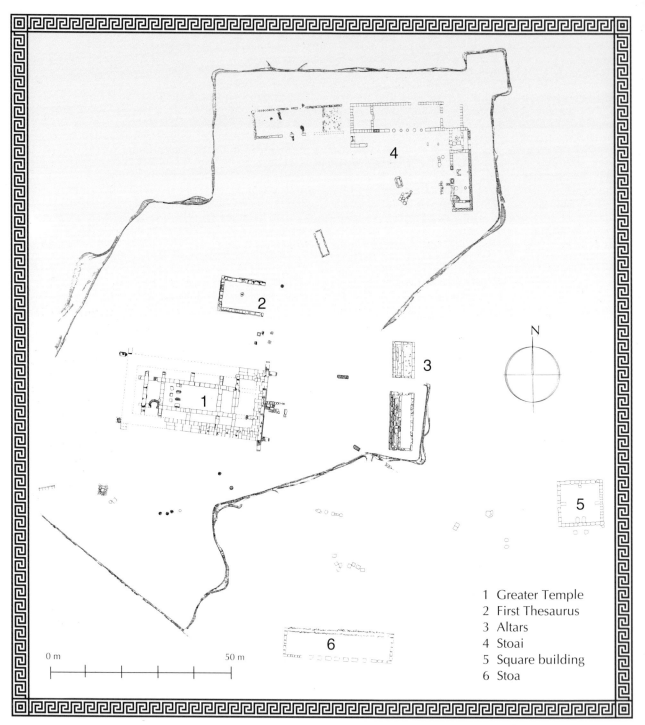

N

1 Greater Temple
2 First Thesaurus
3 Altars
4 Stoai
5 Square building
6 Stoa

0 m          50 m

*Plan of the Heraion of Foce del Sele.*

# HERAION OF FOCE DEL SELE

The remains of the *Heraion* of Foce del Sele stand on the left bank of the river Sele, about 10 km. north of Poseidonia. This important sanctuary dedicated to Hera was already cited by ancient sources (Pliny, Strabo, Solinus) for its mythical origins, which went back to one of Jason's stopovers in his travels in search of the golden fleece. With the passage of the centuries even the memory of the site of this place of worship, which had been swallowed up by the marshes, was lost. Not until 1934, thanks to the studies of Paola Zancani Montuoro and Umberto Zanotti Bianco, did its buildings begin to return to light. The origins of the sanctuary are closely related to the foundation of Poseidonia and it marks the extreme northern limit of the territory, bordering with the Etruscanized region north of the Sele. Originally the sanctuary consisted solely of porticoes and an ash altar. It was consecrated to the cult of the Argive Hera, venerated in all her multiple aspects of mother goddess and bride, protectress of fertility and nature and as a warrior goddess.

Around 570/560 B.C. the so-called first *thesaurus* was built, a small temple of which only three sides have survived, rectangular in form, with four columns on the facade. The two anta capitals of the *pronaos* and the famous metopes in the Museum are from the facades. The building was thought by the discoverers to be a votive repository offered by the inhabitants of *Siris* (now Policoro), but this is no longer considered acceptable. The end of the 6th century B.C. was the moment of the sanctuary's greatest vitality. Two podium altars and the great temple of Hera were built. Originally the temple had 8 columns on the front and 17 on the long sides, but today nothing is left but the foundations, built with great care and reinforced in various points to ensure greater stability. A few metopes from the Doric frieze in sandstone, sculptured in relief with figures of dancing maidens, have come to light as well as part of the sima or gutter, also in sandstone, with lion-headed spouts. At the end of the 5th century B.C. all the buildings in the sanctuary were damaged in a violent fire, presumably with the arrival in Poseidonia of the Lucanians, who however built another portico and the so-called Square Building here in the course of the 4th century B.C. utilizing elements of the older monuments. Whether the Square Building was sacred or civil is still a matter of debate among scholars. Only the Greater Temple was restored in this period, while the *thesaurus* was radically despoiled. As revealed by the variety and quantity of the votive material dedicated here, the sanctuary flourished in the 4th century B.C. and throughout the Hellenistic age. That slow process of decline of the place of worship, which began with the romanization of Paestum, came to a head between the last century of the republic and the first of the empire. The events that marked the end of this sacred site included an attack by Cilician pirates (1st cent. B.C.) as mentioned by Plutarch, serious damage inflicted by the earthquake of 62 A.D. and the eruption of Vesuvius in 79 A.D. Sporadically frequented up to the Hadrianic period, in the Middle Ages it became a source of material for a limekiln set up on the southern side of what had once been the great temple of Hera at Foce del Sele.

*Heraion of Foce del Sele: detail of the foundations of the Greater Temple.*

Velia, the acropolis: the Angevin tower built on the foundations of the temple.

Velia: Porta Rosa.

# VELIA

Velia lies about 40 km. south of Paestum. The history of this Greek colony is well known. Herodotus (5th cent. B.C.) and Strabo (imperial age), who refers to an older account by Antiochus of Syracuse, tell us that the inhabitants of Phocaea, a city in Asia Minor, hard pressed by the Persians, moved to Corsica around 545 B.C., where other Phocaeans had founded the city of Alalia about twenty years earlier.

In the following five years the newcomers per-formed acts of piratry, arousing the ire of the Etruscans and the Carthaginians, allied to defend their interests on the Tyrrhenian. The Phocaeans were badly defeated in a naval encounter, and the survivors, with 20 ships, succeeded in reaching Reggio, where a native of Poseidonia (see p.3) indi-cated the site where a city could be founded. The new colony, named after a spring nearby, was called *Hyele* and then *Elea*, which turned into Velia in Roman times.

*Velia: view of the southern quarter.*

The city is famous for its philosophers Parmenides and Zeno, who provided it with a solid constitution and good laws, thus enabling Velia to defeat the Poseidonians and the Lucanians. Even when Lucania later took over the entire region, it never succeeded in conquering Velia. Always a faithful ally of Rome, the pleasant climate made it a favorite vacation site, where Cicero also sojourned.

When the two harbors silted up (the area of the southern harbor was apparently already being used as a cemetery in the imperial age) the city declined. In the Middle Ages the inhabited center was limited to the hill, where the imposing Angevin tower was to rise in the 13th century.

Elea or Velia stood on a promontory which originally faced directly on the sea with the acropolis on high, while the two residential quarters, connected by a road, spread out on the slopes.

Beginning our visit with the acropolis, on the left one can observe the remains of houses, mostly with a single room, built in polygonal blocks of sandstone. These are the oldest dwellings in the city, cut, around 480 B.C., by the building of a great terrace wall in squared blocks, after which the upper part of the residential area was set aside as a sacred space. Only part of the foundations of the large temple which rose here are still visible, for the tower was built on the site of the cella. Further south lies a large rectangular building, perhaps meant for the votive offerings of the sanctuary. A small theater was also built in the 3rd century B.C. and traces of the tiers still remain.

East of the acropolis, an open space marks a zone where numerous shrines, altars and sacred areas dedicated to various divinities were situated, as is clear from the inscriptions found here and preserved in the little church nearby, which also has a small *antiquarium* open to the public.

The walls of the city skirt the area: note the earliest phase, in small blocks, and the later one in large squared blocks. One of the square fortification towers stands on the way to the far end of the hill. The open space reached by passing over the arch of Porta Rosa (see p.74) contains the foundations of a shrine of Hellenistic date.

A bit further on is another tower, known as Castelluccio, to which the fortification that enclosed the southern quarter was connected. Of the city's two quarters, only the southern one is open to the public, with the entrance at Porta Marina.

On the right are funeral enclosures of Roman times. It is to be recalled that when the city was founded there was a harbor in this area and when it silted up at the end of the 4th century B.C., the result of a flood and the gradual withdrawal of the coastline, the entire zone was enclosed by a stretch of wall and urbanized.

Further on the road skirts, on the right, two blocks with late 4th century B.C. dwellings before passing through a gate in the city walls. The large circular well then encountered was presumably, to judge from the material found and letters engraved on a rock closeby, part of a sanctuary to Eros.

Near the well is a bath building of the 2nd century A.D. with a mosaic pavement of marine subjects in the *frigidarium*.

Further on, in a southeast direction, a large building, which occupies the space of an entire pre-existing block, is interpreted as the site of the imperial cult. Datable to the 1st century A.D., it consists of two triple porticoes of which one rests on a vaulted ambulatory or *cryptoporticus*.

Turning back, opposite the baths, a paved road, datable in its layout to the Hellenistic period, leads past a *nymphaeum* of imperial times, in which the bases of Ionic columns dating to the 5th century B.C. have been reused, to a porticoed area, previously identified as the agora or part of a complex of monumental fountains which received water from the *Hyele* spring.

*Velia: view of the southern quarter: in the foreground the sacred well.*

*Velia: some views of the southern quarter.*

Nearby a bath building of the 3rd century B.C. has recently been excavated and restored. One of the rooms contains mosaics in tesserae, one of the oldest known to depict figures.

At the end of the paved road is Porta Rosa, preceded by an older gate, a residue of the first fortification phase (around 500 B.C.). Porta Rosa is really none other than the monumental layout of the bottleneck through which passed the road that led to the northern quarter of the city, almost completely unexplored. Two uprights support a round arch built of sandstone ashlars and surmounted by a relieving arch, at present filled in. Dating to the second half of the 4th century B.C., it seems to be the oldest extant example of an arch built in ashlars in *Magna Graecia*.

75

Velia: the road that leads to Porta Rosa.

Velia: the baths.

Velia: detail of the baths.

Velia, acropolis: the tower and the remains of the theater.

# PAESTUM

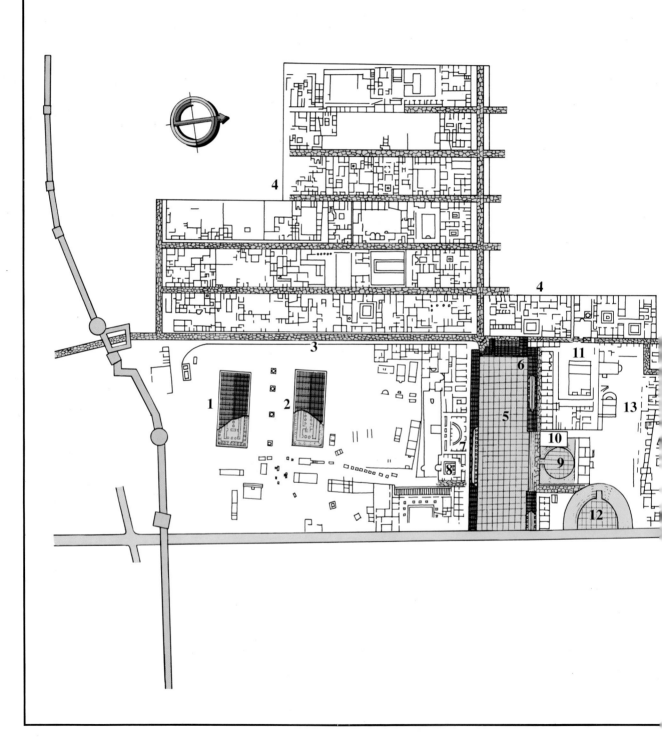

1 Basilica
2 Temple of Neptune
3 "Via Sacra"
4 Residential quarters
5 Forum
6 Lares shrine
7 Curia
8 Macellum
9 Comitium
10 Italic Temple
11 Piscina
12 Amphitheater
13 Southern portico of the agora
14 Cenotaph-Heroon
15 Bouleuterion
16 Temple of Ceres

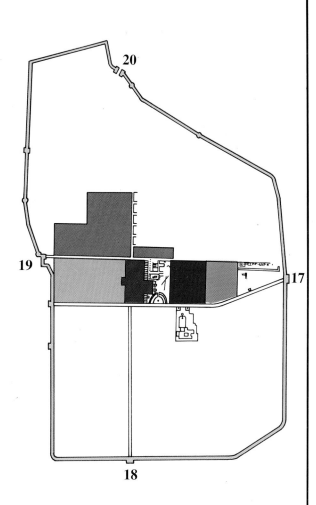

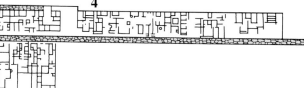

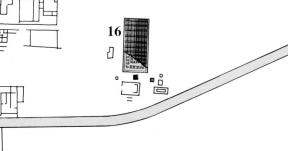

■ Southern sanctuary

■ Forum

■ Agora

■ Northern sanctuary

■ Residential quarters

■ Walls, towers and gates

17 Porta Aurea
18 Porta Sirena
19 Porta Giustizia
20 Porta Marina

# GLOSSARY

ABACUS = a rectangular slab forming the crowning member of the Doric capital.

AGORA = the town square in a Greek city, gathering place and center of political and economic life.

APSE = curved projection of one side of a room.

ASKOS = schematized duck-shaped vase.

ATRIUM = central court in a Roman house, sometimes surrounded by a portico, on which all the rooms opened to take light.

BLACK-FIGURE = technique for decorating pottery in which the figures are in black against a red ground, initially preceding red-figure.

BOULEUTERION = meeting place of the boule, or citizens' council (senate) in a Greek city.

CAPITAL = the crowning feature of a column or pilaster, consisting of an echinus and abacus.

CAVEA = the space occupied by tiers inside assembly buildings, theaters and amphitheaters.

CENOTAPH = (Gk. "empty tomb"). A symbolic funerary monument erected in memory of an eminent person or a hero.

DORIC = the simplest order of Greek architecture, characterized by the shape of the capitals and the columns without a base.

DORIC FRIEZE = in temples of the Doric order it is the middle division of the entablature, above the architrave, composed of metopes and triglyphs

GEISON = the raking cornice of the pediment.

GYMNASIUM = Greek name for the place where youths performed their gymnastic exercises.

HELLENISTIC = the culture which resulted from the fusion of Greek and oriental customs, language and culture after the conquests of Alexander the Great. Conventionally set between 323 and 40 B.C.

HERAION = sanctuary or temple dedicated to Hera.

HEROON = building dedicated to the cult of a hero or a figure who became a hero after his death.

HYDRIA = a vase with three handles (two horizontal and one vertical), in bronze or pottery, which was used to fetch water.

HYPOGEUM = underground.

IMPLUVIUM = rectangular basin in the floor of the atrium of a house, to collect the water that entered from the corresponding opening in the roof.

IONIC = order of Greek architecture, characterized by volute capitals and columns with a molded base.

KANTHAROS = cup for drinking, with two tall vertical handles.

KLINE = couch used at banquets.

KOTTABOS = game played during banquets in which wine was thrown from a cup into a crater set at the center of the room.

KRATER = a large deep bowl with a wide mouth and two handles, chiefly used for mixing wine and water.

KYLIX = low bowl for drinking with two handles.

LEBES GAMIKOS = nuptial lebes.

LEBETE = large bronze vessel which rested on a tripod. Numerous examples offered as votive gifts in the sanctuary of Olympia are known. In South Italian red-figure pottery the term is used to designate a type of vase with an ovoid body and two vertical handles, with a lid that is often composed of several superposed elements.

LEKANE = low shallow bowl with two handles and a lid.

LEKYTHOS = an oval flask with a lip and a single vertical handle, used for unguents and perfume oil.

LUCANIAN = in Paestum the period from the end of the 5th cent. to 273 B.C.

METOPE = flat slab between the triglyphs on the Doric frieze, sometimes painted or sculptured.

OINOCHOE = pitcher with a wide mouth and a vertical handle, used for pouring wine.

OLPE = bellied flask, with one handle, cylindrical neck and flaring lip.

OPISTHODOMOS = the room which adjoined the temple chamber itself at the rear, often serving for the preservation of the most important or precious votive offerings.

PATERA = shallow wide bowl in pottery or metal, without handles.

PELIKE = a type of low amphora with a swollen body.

PERISTASIS = the external colonnade of the temple and the covered area around the cella.

PERISTYLE = in the Roman house, an inner court surrounded by columns.

PRONAOS = in the temple, the open porch or vestibule in front of the cella, often with pillars in front.

RED-FIGURE POTTERY = style of painting in which the figures are in red, with details drawn in with a brush, against a dark background.

SIMA = gutter.

STOA = portico. In sanctuaries, the semicovered areas where the faithful were sheltered.

SYMPOSIUM = drinking bout.

TEMENOS = the area dedicated to the sanctuary, generally surrounded by an enclosing wall.

THESAURUS = in the sanctuaries, a small building, sometimes in the form of a shrine, used as a repository for offerings to the gods.

TRIGLYPH = a surface ornamented with three parallel vertical channels set between the metopes in the Doric frieze.

TYMPANUM = the slab set in the opening of the pediment.

VILLANOVAN CULTURE = the culture which developed in the Iron Age and assumed various regional nuances. In Campania its appearance was connected to a vast process of expansion by peoples of Etruscan origin in centers such as Capua and Pontecagnano. The name comes from Villanova, near Bologna, where this culture was first identified.